be happy

EACH DAY

A JOURNAL FOR
LIFELONG HAPPINESS
Domonique Bertolucci

---

hardie grant books

CHOOSE
HAPPINESS.

MOST PEOPLE ARE LOOKING FOR
HAPPINESS IN ALL THE WRONG PLACES.

They think it's something they can achieve or acquire, that they'll be happy when they've done this or got that.

They're looking to discover the one thing that will guarantee their happiness, so they can relax and enjoy the ride. But that one thing is never what you think it's going to be.

Life is full of ups and downs. Some things will go well for you and turn out exactly the way you want them to, and others perhaps not so much.

The truth is, there is only one thing you can do that is guaranteed to make you happy, and that is to decide to be happy. It really is as simple as that.

DON'T BE DECEIVED BY THE SIMPLICITY OF THIS JOURNAL.

Throughout this journal you will find quotes to inspire you and actions to guide you.

You will also find plenty of blank space to capture the thoughts, hopes and dreams you have for your life.

There is no right or wrong way to fill in the blanks or specific order you need to follow for the actions.

Just close your eyes, breathe deeply and trust that the page you open will be exactly the one you needed to see.

Used regularly, this journal has the power to transform your life.

If you want to find out more about living your happiest and most fulfilling life, visit domoniquebertolucci.com/life and download the *Brilliant Life Handbook*.

HAPPINESS IS A CHOICE. CHOOSE TO BE HAPPY AND YOU WILL BE.

When you wake up each morning take a
moment to think about the kind of life you want
to have. Write down five things you can do that
will make this a reality.

1.

2.

3.

4.

5.

EVEN THOUGH LIFE MAY PRESENT YOU
WITH ALL MANNER OF UPS AND DOWNS,
HAVING THE RIGHT ATTITUDE WILL
ENSURE YOUR DAY WILL BE A GOOD ONE,
REGARDLESS OF WHAT IT IS YOU ARE GIVEN
TO WORK WITH.

Describe the mindset you want to adopt today.

*Make this even more powerful by using positive,
present tense and personal language.

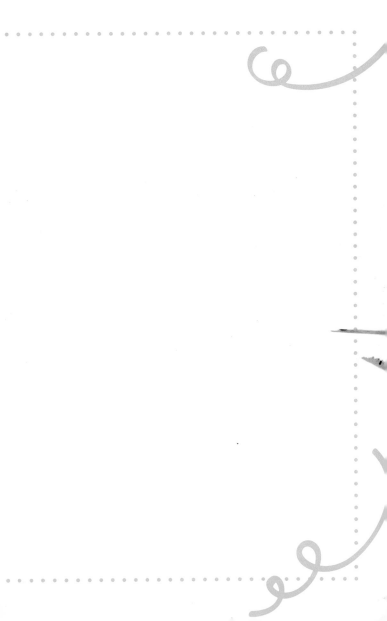

BELIEVE IN YOURSELF, BELIEVE IN YOUR DREAMS AND BELIEVE IN YOUR RIGHT TO ACHIEVE YOUR DREAMS.

———

BEING GENEROUS
IS NOT JUST
ABOUT THE
DECISIONS YOU
MAKE WITH
YOUR WALLET.
BEING GENEROUS
WITH YOUR TIME
AND ENERGY
IS JUST AS
IMPORTANT.

———

WHEN LIFE GETS BUSY IT'S EASY TO PUT OFF GETTING IN TOUCH WITH FAMILY OR FRIENDS WITH THE EXCUSE THAT 'THERE ARE NEVER ENOUGH HOURS IN THE DAY'.

Make a list of the five most important people in your life and make a commitment to connect with them today.

1.

2.

3.

4.

5.

*It doesn't need to be a long phone call or lengthy letter. Just a simple message that says 'I love you' or 'You're special to me' can make all the difference in someone's world.

ALTHOUGH HAPPINESS IS A STATE OF BEING, IT STILL USUALLY REQUIRES SOME DOING IF IT IS TO BE LASTING IN YOUR LIFE.

Think of something you can do that is
guaranteed to put you in a good mood.
It doesn't have to be a grand gesture or lofty
goal... sometimes it's the simplest ideas that
are the most powerful.

Today I will...

Take a minute to think about any limiting
beliefs or negative self-talk you currently
engage in and write down the new, positive
and encouraging thoughts you plan to
adopt instead.

LEARNING
FROM THE
PAST CAN HELP
YOU MOVE
FORWARD.
LINGERING IN
THE PAST WILL
ONLY HOLD
YOU BACK.

Make a note of three insights, light-bulb
moments or lessons you've gained from
your recent experiences.

PERFECTION IS A LOST CAUSE. FOCUS YOUR ENERGY ON BEING THE BEST YOU CAN BE.

Think back to a challenging experience and reflect on what you learned.

*When you are able to focus on what you've gained, you'll be able to turn every experience into a positive one, regardless of the outcome.

—

WORRYING IS
A WASTE OF
ENERGY.
FOCUS INSTEAD
ON THE OUTCOME
YOU WANT, AND
DO WHAT YOU
CAN TO MAKE IT
HAPPEN.

—

Think of something that has been worrying or concerning you lately. Close your eyes and imagine a future where, instead of your worry becoming real, you get your perfect outcome.

Now open your eyes and write down exactly how that made you feel.

Make a list of five things you want to have more of, less of, or do differently in your life.

1.

2.

3.

4.

5.

CHOOSE YOUR
BATTLES WISELY.
UNLESS YOU
HAVE A HIGH
CHANCE OF
VICTORY, SPARE
YOUR ENERGY AND
WALK AWAY.

—

BEING HAPPY IS NOT A PRIVILEGE – IT IS SOMETHING EVERYONE DESERVES.

—

Make a list of five things that will help you
remember that you really are worth, and
truly deserve, to live a happy and fulfilling life.

1.

2.

3.

4.

5.

—

COMMIT TO BEING HAPPY AND MAKE CHOICES THAT SUPPORT YOUR COMMITMENT.

—

LIVE YOUR LIFE WITH COURAGEOUS INTEGRITY. DO THE RIGHT THING, NOT THE EASY THING.

Include the things you believe in, are passionate about, or value most and make a declaration about how you want your life to be.

* Want to see an example of a personal manifesto? Check out the inside cover of this journal.

Plan out your day, making sure you allow time to do something just for you.

TIME	PLAN

YOUR EXPECTATIONS DETERMINE YOUR EXPERIENCE. EXPECT THE BEST FROM LIFE AND YOU WILL USUALLY GET IT.

Keep smiling until you feel a sense of calm and
contentment wash over you. Now take a minute
to write down how you feel.

* Carry this feeling with you for the rest of
your day.

DON'T TAKE YOUR HAPPINESS FOR GRANTED. BE PROACTIVE ABOUT MAINTAINING AND SUSTAINING IT IN YOUR LIFE.

Every time you take money out of your wallet today, remind yourself how fortunate you are just to be able to do so.

I am lucky to be able to spend my money on...

**DON'T DENY
YOUR EMOTIONS
AND FORCE
YOURSELF
TO SMILE WHEN
YOU FEEL
LIKE CRYING.**

DON'T FALL INTO THE HABIT OF KEEPING
SCORE IN YOUR FRIENDSHIPS. INSTEAD
OF KEEPING TRACK OF WHO PHONED
WHOM LAST OR WHOSE TURN IT IS TO
PAY FOR COFFEE, MAKE A POINT OF
BEING THE FIRST TO ACT, NOT THE LAST.

Make a list of your three most treasured
friends and think of something nice you can
do for them.

—

JUST BECAUSE
THERE ARE THINGS
YOU STILL WANT,
THAT DOESN'T MEAN
YOU CAN'T FEEL
GRATITUDE FOR ALL
THE WEALTH
AND ABUNDANCE
ALREADY IN
YOUR LIFE.

—

Make a list of ten things you are grateful for in your life.

1.

2.

3.

4.

5.

6.

7.

8.

9.

10.

While it might not be possible to make yourself your number-one priority every single day, it's important to have your own needs met if you want to have the energy it takes to be there for everyone else.

Today I will...

because it makes me happy.

Today I will...

because it makes me happy.

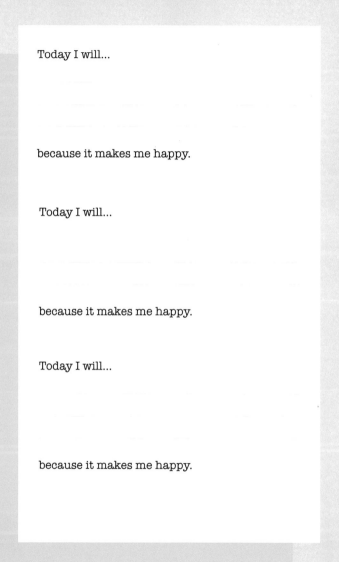

Today I will...

because it makes me happy.

Today I will...

because it makes me happy.

Today I will...

because it makes me happy.

—

YOU ONLY
HAVE ONE LIFE.
MAKE SURE
YOURS IS
ONE YOU'RE
HAPPY TO BE
LIVING.

—

Make a list of ten simple things that make you happy.

1.

2.

3.

4.

5.

6.

7.

8.

9.

10.

* This is not supposed to be a bucket list, but a list of simple everyday things you can do that bring joy or happiness into your life.

LOOK FOR
THE JOY IN
EACH AND
EVERY DAY.
JUST BECAUSE
IT ISN'T
IMMEDIATELY
OBVIOUS
DOESN'T MEAN
IT'S NOT
THERE.

YOUR
SELF-ESTEEM
IS ONE OF
YOUR MOST
PRECIOUS
POSSESSIONS.
TREAT YOURS
WITH THE
RESPECT
IT DESERVES.

LISTEN TO YOUR INNER DIALOGUE AND
MAKE THE COMMITMENT TODAY TO ONLY
EVER SPEAK TO YOURSELF WITH KINDNESS,
PATIENCE AND LOVE.

I will be kind to
myself when...

I will be patient
with myself when...

I love myself
because...

My goal is...

I will...

to make it happen...

My goal is...

I will...

to make it happen...

My goal is...

I will...

to make it happen...

My goal is...

I will...

to make it happen...

THINK OF A TIME IN THE PAST WHEN YOU HAVE JUDGED OR CRITICISED YOURSELF. MAKE THE DECISION TO FORGIVE YOURSELF FOR WHATEVER IT WAS YOU DID OR FAILED TO DO.

I forgive
myself for...

I forgive
myself for...

I forgive
myself for...

—

THERE'S NOTHING
WRONG WITH
WANTING
EVERYTHING THAT
LIFE CAN OFFER,
AS LONG AS YOU
DON'T ALLOW IT TO
STAND IN THE
WAY OF YOUR
HAPPINESS.

—

In order to be happy I need ....

- ☐
- ☐
- ☐
- ☐
- ☐
- ☐
- ☐
- ☐
- ☐

* When you understand the difference between 'want' and 'need', you will realise how rich your life really is.

MOST PEOPLE
ARE FINE WITH
'FINE' AND OKAY
WITH 'OKAY'.
IF YOU WANT
TO BE THE BEST
YOU CAN BE,
MAKE SURE
YOU'RE NOT.

It doesn't matter if this isn't how you felt
yesterday, or if you don't yet have the
confidence to know you will feel this way
tomorrow. Just begin each day with
this thought in mind and watch your
self-belief grow.

I believe in myself because...

I believe I can...

I believe I will...

UNLESS YOU HAVE
A CRYSTAL BALL,
YOU DON'T KNOW
HOW THE FUTURE IS
GOING TO UNFOLD.
FOCUS ON THE
THINGS YOU CAN
INFLUENCE, AND
DON'T FRET ABOUT
THE REST.

IN THE GAME OF LIFE THE MOST IMPORTANT THING IS JUST SHOWING UP AND DOING YOUR BEST. DESCRIBE WHAT YOUR PERSONAL BEST LOOKS LIKE IN THE CORE AREAS OF YOUR LIFE.

When I do my best I am...

—

**SOMETIMES
BEING HAPPY
WILL REQUIRE
SOME DIFFICULT
CONVERSATIONS.
SOME OF THOSE
CONVERSATIONS
WILL BE WITH
YOURSELF.**

—

Draft a pep talk that you can give yourself next time you find yourself or your happiness slumping.

DON'T BE AFRAID TO TAKE A CHANCE. THE WORST THAT CAN HAPPEN IS THAT YOU DON'T SUCCEED... THIS TIME.

If everything you really wanted to do,
be or have was possible, what would your
life look like?

—

FOCUS ON
WHAT MATTERS.
HONOUR YOUR
VALUES AND
MAKE DECISIONS
THAT ARE ALIGNED
WITH THEM.

—

Make a list of your core values or the things that matter most in your life.

☐ I commit to living a life that is in alignment with my values.

One of the easiest ways to eliminate your negative self-talk is to create affirmations: positive, personal and present-tense statements that boost your self-esteem while reprogramming your subconscious thoughts.

Try it – it works!

I am...

I am...

I am...

THERE'S NOTHING WRONG WITH ENJOYING LIFE'S LUXURIES AS LONG AS YOUR HAPPINESS ISN'T CONTINGENT ON THEM.

—

IT'S HARD
TO BE PRESENT
WHEN YOUR
ATTENTION IS
SUFFERING
INFORMATION
OVERLOAD.
SWITCH OFF
AND JUST
SIT STILL.

—

Make a list of all the different ways you can find
or create silence in your day.

* As few as five minutes can leave you feeling so
refreshed and re-energised, you'll think you've
been recharging for five hours!

AS LONG
AS YOU
DO YOUR BEST,
YOUR BEST
WILL ALWAYS
BE GOOD
ENOUGH.

BEING
OPTIMISTIC
ISN'T ABOUT
BELIEVING
NOTHING CAN
GO WRONG.
AN OPTIMIST
ACKNOWLEDGES
WHAT CAN GO
WRONG, BUT
EXPECTS THINGS
TO GO RIGHT.

Think of a goal you are working on or something you want to achieve and make a note of three things you can confidently do that will bring you closer to it.

1.

2.

3.

NO MATTER HOW MUCH YOU CARE ABOUT SOMEONE, YOU CAN'T TAKE RESPONSIBILITY FOR THEIR HAPPINESS.

TO BE HAPPY,
YOU NEED TO DO
THE RIGHT THING
FOR YOU, EVEN
WHEN IT FEELS
LIKE THE
HARDEST THING
IN THE WORLD.

Think of a time when you had to make a difficult decision or were faced with a challenging situation. What did you learn from that experience?

THE HAPPIEST, MOST SUCCESSFUL PEOPLE BELIEVE IN THEMSELVES UNCONDITIONALLY. THEY KNOW THEY CAN DO, BE AND HAVE ALL THAT THEY WANT IN LIFE.

BE THERE WHEN
YOU'RE THERE.
DON'T TRY TO
JUGGLE ALL
THE ROLES
IN YOUR LIFE.
FOCUS ON THE
ROLE YOU ARE
PLAYING AND
DO IT TO THE
BEST OF
YOUR ABILITY.

Make a list of all the different roles you play in life: friend, daughter, parent, brother, employee, etc. Now make a note of how you can be more present when you are in each role.

Choose a simple thought to begin each day with
to remind yourself of this.

MOST OF THE THINGS YOU FIND YOURSELF WANTING WILL HAVE LITTLE OR NO BEARING ON THE HAPPINESS IN YOUR LIFE.

—

SO MANY PEOPLE SABOTAGE THEIR OWN CHANCES FOR HAPPINESS. DON'T BE ONE OF THEM.

—

THINK ABOUT THE MOST COMMON WAYS THAT YOU LET YOURSELF DOWN OR SABOTAGE YOUR INTENTIONS. WHAT CAN YOU DO TO PREVENT YOURSELF FROM DOING THIS IN FUTURE?

IT'S EASY TO BE BRAVE WHEN EVERYTHING IS GOING YOUR WAY. WHEN THE GOING GETS TOUGH, IT TAKES COURAGE TO FOLLOW THE PATH YOU BELIEVE IN.

Take a minute to write the pep talk you will give yourself next time you feel like giving up or giving in. This way, you'll have it handy when you need it.

IF YOU WANT TO BE THE BEST YOU CAN BE, DON'T JUDGE ANYONE: NOT EVEN YOURSELF.

MULTITASKING IS STRESSFUL.
YOU WILL GET THINGS DONE
MUCH FASTER IF YOU DO
THEM ONE AT A TIME.

Make a list of three essential things that you need to get done today and do them one at a time until they are completed.

1.

2.

3.

* Remember, ten per cent of ten things isn't one hundred per cent of anything.

THERE IS NO SUCH THING AS 'NO CHOICE'. THERE ARE ALWAYS OTHER OPTIONS. EXPLORE YOURS.

DON'T DEPEND ON OTHERS TO FUEL YOUR SELF-BELIEF. DEVELOP YOUR SELF-BELIEF SO THAT IT BECOMES SELF-SUSTAINING.

Remind yourself each day that you are good enough.
You don't need anyone to tell you for it to be true.

Make a list of your ten best qualities or attributes.

1.

2.

3.

4.

5.

6.

7.

8.

9.

10.

*If you can't fill in the whole list today, don't worry.
Come back and add to it whenever you can.

TAKE A MINUTE TO VISUALISE WHAT YOUR
IDEAL DAY WOULD BE LIKE. MENTALLY WALK
THROUGH YOUR DAY FROM THE MOMENT
YOU WAKE UP TO WHEN YOU GO TO BED
AT NIGHT AND TRY TO PICTURE AS MANY
DETAILS AS YOU POSSIBLY CAN.

Now write down all the key elements of your
vision and commit to making them a reality in
your life.

IT'S ONLY
WHEN YOUR
ACTIONS AND
WORDS ARE
ALIGNED THAT
YOU CAN
ACHIEVE
YOUR TRUE
POTENTIAL.

Think of three things that you can do this week that will take you closer to your goal.

1.

2.

3.

I commit to completing these actions by...

DATE:

REMEMBER TO AFFORD YOURSELF THE SAME GENEROSITY YOU GIVE TO OTHERS.

TAKE A MINUTE TO THINK OF ALL THE
THINGS IN YOUR LIFE THAT YOU HAVE
SUCCEEDED AT OR ACHIEVED.

Make time today to acknowledge all that you
have achieved, no matter how long ago it was.

—

IT DOESN'T
MATTER IF YOU
GIVE THANKS
TO GOD, THE
UNIVERSE OR
EVEN JUST
YOURSELF.
ALL THAT
MATTERS IS THAT
YOU REMEMBER
TO SAY
'THANK YOU'.

—

Make a list of all the things you are grateful for in your life. Read this list over and allow yourself to appreciate fully the wealth and abundance in your life.

**BE HONEST
WITH YOURSELF.
YOU CAN'T BE
THE BEST YOU
CAN BE UNLESS
YOU KNOW
WHO YOU
REALLY ARE.**

—

UNLESS YOU
HAVE THE
COURAGE TO
SAY 'NO' TO
THE THINGS YOU
DON'T WANT,
IT'S HARDER TO
SAY 'YES' TO THE
THINGS THAT YOU
DO WANT.

—

Make a list of all the things you want to stop,
give up or have less of in your life.

I commit to having more of what I want
in my life and less of what I don't want.

Instead of spending your time thinking about
what is missing, make the decision today to
relax in the knowledge that while your life
might not be perfect, it's already pretty good.

My life is good because...

—

REMIND YOURSELF: IF IT WON'T MATTER IN TEN YEARS, IT DOESN'T MATTER TODAY.

—

—

IT'S OKAY
TO ASPIRE
TO A BETTER LIFE,
BUT DON'T
LET IT STOP YOU
FROM ENJOYING
THE LIFE
YOU ALREADY
HAVE.

—

Take a few minutes to picture your life through the eyes of a stranger. If someone who wasn't from your world discovered your life, what would they think?

Describe your life through their eyes.

Make a list of five things you can do that will
mean you are being the best you can be.

1.

2.

3.

4.

5.

DON'T RELY
ON THE
OPINIONS
OF OTHERS.
ONLY YOU
WILL KNOW
WHAT IS RIGHT
FOR YOU.

—

GIVE THE PEOPLE YOU LOVE THE BEST OF YOU, NOT THE WORST.

—

IT'S EASY TO TAKE THE MOST IMPORTANT PEOPLE IN YOUR LIFE FOR GRANTED, LEAVING THEM AT THE BOTTOM OF YOUR TO-DO LIST. AT THE END OF YOUR LIFE, THE PEOPLE WHOM YOU'VE LOVED AND WHO HAVE LOVED YOU WILL PROVE TO BE ONE OF YOUR GREATEST SOURCES OF HAPPINESS.

These are the most important people in my life...

☐ I commit to making them my priority.

CHOOSE TO BE HAPPY. IT'S THE ONLY SENSIBLE OPTION.

Domonique Bertolucci is the best-selling author of
The Happiness Code: Ten Keys to Being the Best You Can Be
and the closely guarded secret of some of the world's
most successful people.

Passionate about helping people to get the life they want
and love the life they've got, Domonique has a client list that
reads like a who's who of CEOs and business identities, award-
winning entrepreneurs and celebrities. Her workshops and
online courses are attended by people from all walks of life,
from all around the world. Domonique helps her clients define
their personal happiness prescription and then shows them
exactly how to make it their reality.

Since writing her first book, *Your Best Life*, in 2006,
Domonique has become a world-renowned life strategist and
happiness coach. More than ten million people have seen, read
or heard her advice.

Domonique currently lives in London but her reach is truly
global. In addition to her Australian clients, she has coached
people in London, Amsterdam, Paris, New York, Toronto,
Singapore and Hong Kong. Her weekly newsletter,
Love Your Life, has readers in more than 60 countries.

When she is not working, Domonique's favourite ways to spend
her time are with her husband and two children, reading a good
book and keeping up the great Italian tradition of feeding the
people that you love.

Keep in touch with Domonique at:

domoniquebertolucci.com
facebook.com/domoniquebertolucci
instagram.com/domoniquebertolucci

Sign up for Domonique's free life-coaching course at:
domoniquebertolucci.com/life

Other books by Domonique

The Happiness Code: Ten keys to being the best you can be

Love Your Life: 100 ways to start living the life you deserve

100 Days Happier: Daily inspiration for life-long happiness

Less is More: 101 ways to simplify your life

The Kindness Pact: 8 promises to make you feel good about who you are and the life you live

The Daily Promise: 100 ways to feel happy about your life

Other journals in this series

Live More Each Day: A journal to discover what really matters

Business Development Director *Melanie Gray*
Designer *Maeve Bargman*
Production Director *Vincent Smith*
Production Controller *Jessica Otway*

Published in 2018 by **Hardie Grant Books**, an imprint of
Hardie Grant Publishing

Hardie Grant Books *(Melbourne)*
Building 1, 658 Church Street
Richmond, Victoria 3121

Hardie Grant Books *(London)*
52–54 Southwark Street
London SE1 1UN

hardiegrant.com

Copyright text © *Domonique Bertolucci 2018*
Copyright design © *Quadrille 2018*

ISBN 978 1 74379 4296
Printed in China